WHAT ON EARTH?
WATER

Isabel Thomas
Pau Morgan

Take your grown-up on a water hunt on page 6.

Contents

Read about the greedy frog Tiddalik on page 10.

What is water?

Water and the Weather

Find out all about the water cycle on page 30.

Watery World

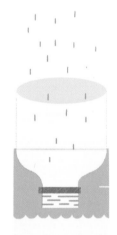

Discover how a Bactrian camel saves water in the desert on page 49.

Water and Nature

Water and our Planet

See how you can have fun with water on page 58.

Water poems

Think about water – where does it come from? Can you write a poem about water?

Water, water, everywhere.

Water, water, everywhere,
waste no water anywhere.

Sow a seed and water it,
see a lovely plant grow from it.

Raindrops dripping from the trees,
a drink for thirsty birds and bees.

Fill your glass up at the sink
and drink and drink and drink.

Water, water, everywhere,
waste no water anywhere.

The rain

Pitter-patter, raindrops,
falling from the sky.
Here is my umbrella
to keep me safe and dry!
When the rain is over,
and the Sun begins to glow,
little flowers start to bud,
and grow and grow and grow!

A watery world

It falls from the sky and flows over the ground. It rushes from taps and trickles down windows. Water covers most of the Earth's surface.

From raindrops on a leaf...

...to puddles in the street...

...and oceans wide and deep...

...water is EVERYWHERE!

Ask your grown-up to take you on a water hunt. How many different places can you find water near your home?

Whether you love to get wet...

...or prefer to stay dry...

...we all need water to keep us alive.

Water rules

Water is special. It follows its own rules. Try these activities to find out more about wonderful, weird, wet water!

Toolkit
- Water from a tap
- Jug
- Plastic containers of different sizes
- Small plastic bag
- Sugar

What to do

1 Put some water in a jug. Now pour it into another container. What happens?

2 Tip a little sugar and a little water on a flat surface. What happens? When you pour sugar, it makes a pile. When you pour water, it makes a puddle. Now put two drops of water close to each other. What happens when they touch?

Water is runny and easy to pour. It changes shape. It is a liquid.

Water clings together.

3 Dip your hand into a cup of sugar. Pull it out again. Then try it with water. What do you notice?

4 Poke a small hole in a plastic bag. Pour some water in. What happens?

5 Fill the bottom of a clear bowl with sugar. Hold it over this page. Can you still see the pictures? Then try it with water. What do you notice?

6 Put some warm water in a cup. Add a teaspoon of sugar. What happens?

Sugar mixes so well with water, that it breaks up into pieces too tiny to see. We say it has **dissolved**.

Tiddalik

Where does water come from? Why are some places dry, when others are wet? In the past, people told stories to try to answer these questions. This is a story told by the Australian Aboriginal people.

Long ago, there was a frog called Tiddalik, who lived next to a billabong (water hole). One hot day he felt thirsty enough to drink the whole billabong – so he did! Tiddalik was greedy and he didn't want to feel thirsty again.

So after draining the billabong, he drank the stream.

Then after draining the stream, he drank the river.

And after draining the river, he drank the lake!

All the water in the land was now in Tiddalik's huge, green belly.

The next day was long and hot. The plants and animals all needed water. But Tiddalik had taken every last drop. The plants turned dry and brown. The animals grew weak.

What shall we do?

We will die without water.

So they asked the wise old wombat.

The wombat had a plan, "We must make Tiddalik open his mouth. We must make him laugh!" So...

the kangaroo told jokes...

the emu pulled funny faces...

...and the eel tied himself in knots.

But Tiddalik's mouth stayed shut. Then the animals heard a tiny voice. It was a platypus. The giant frog looked at her and smiled. The platypus waved her duck's bill. Tiddalik giggled. A drop of water escaped from his mouth. Then the platypus waggled her webbed feet. Tiddalik roared with laughter.

Look at me!

Water came gushing out of Tiddalik's mouth. It filled the rivers, lakes and billabongs. The plants and animals drank and drank and drank. Tiddalik never took more than his fair share of water again.

States of water

Water is the ONLY substance in the world that can be a solid, liquid and a gas at normal temperatures!

Ice is solid water.

Steam is water that has changed into a gas.

This gas is also found in the air all around us. It's even in the air we breathe out. It is called **water vapour**.

Breathe on a window on a cold day!

Toolkit
- Water from a tap
- Small plastic bag
- Ice cube tray

What to do

Water to ice

Fill an ice cube tray with water. Put it in the freezer. The water will cool down and **freeze** into solid ice. Play with the ice. How is it different from liquid water? What happens when the ice gets warmer?

When ice gets warmer, it **melts**. It changes back into water.

Water vapour is invisible.

Water to gas

Put a few drops of water into a plastic bag. Seal the bag so nothing can escape. Put it on a sunny windowsill. The water will warm up and change into a gas.

When I cool the bag down, the water vapour changes back into water!

Gas to water

Cool the water vapour down again by putting the bag in a fridge or freezer. What happens?

Make an iceberg

Make your own iceberg to find out more about ice.

What to do

Toolkit
- Plastic cup
- Freezer
- Pen
- Tap water
- Large, see-through bowl or tub

1 Fill the plastic cup with tap water. Mark the water line.

2 Put the cup in a freezer overnight.

3 Take the cup out of the freezer. Your water has turned to ice. Look at the line you marked.

4 Fill a bowl or tub with cold tap water. Ask your grown-up to help you squeeze the lump of ice out of the cup, into the water.

Biggest iceberg ever!

The biggest iceberg ever seen was the size of Jamaica. It formed in Antarctica, when a huge piece of ice broke off a glacier. The iceberg took twelve years to melt and break apart.

In the Arctic, a floating sheet of ice covers the sea in winter. Underneath, the sea is still liquid water.

Water freezes when it reaches 0°C.

Small icebergs are called bergy bits or growlers.

What happens?

As water freezes it gets bigger and takes up more space. This is why the ice in your cup is above the water line. Ice is lighter than water, so it floats. Real icebergs are just like massive ice cubes, floating in the ocean. Only the tip of an iceberg pokes out above the water. Most is below the water.

It's the tip of the iceberg!

Be a water detective

It's easy to see solid and liquid water, but water vapour is invisible. Be a water detective and look for the clues to see if there really is water in the air.

Stand back, boiling water and steam are very dangerous!

Clue 1: Hot drinks

Watch a grown-up make a hot drink. When water is heated to 100°C, it changes into water vapour very quickly. We say the water is boiling. When the water vapour mixes with cooler air, some of it turns back into tiny drops of liquid water. This is called steam.

Clue 2: Puddles vanish

Puddles don't stay on the ground forever. They vanish over a few hours or days. Some of the water may soak into the ground. The rest turns into water vapour. The puddle doesn't boil. The water changes to a gas slowly using heat from the Sun.

Clue 3: Breathe water

Dragons breath fire, and you breathe... water! Next time you are in a car and it is cool outside, breathe onto the car window. Water vapour in your breath cools down as it hits the cold window and changes back into tiny drops of liquid water.

Clue 4: Make frost

Fill an empty, dry metal cup or container with ice cubes. Put it in a warm room. Watch the outside of the cup.

What happens?

Frost forms on the outside of the cup. Ice has not travelled through the cup. Instead, water vapour in the air around the cup has been cooled very quickly as it touches the cold metal, and has turned to ice.

Cloud in a jar

Find out where clouds come from by making a cloud in a jar.

Toolkit
- Glass jar with a metal lid
- Water
- Measuring jug
- Ice cubes
- Hairspray

What to do

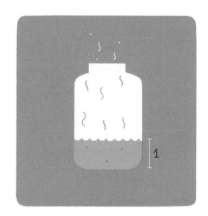

1 Warm up the jar by filling it with warm water (ask your grown-up to do this bit).

2 Turn the metal lid upside down and put a handful of ice cubes inside.

3 Ask your grown-up to tip the warm water out of the jar and then put 1 cm of hot water into the bottom of the jar.

4 Ask your grown-up to squirt a small amount of hairspray into the jar (try not to get it on the sides). Then quickly put the upside-down lid on top of the jar. Watch carefully to see what happens. Can you see a cloud swirling around near the top of the jar?

What happens?

The hot water at the bottom of the jar **evaporates** (turns into a gas). The water vapour is carried up into the air. When it gets near the top of the jar it cools and turns back into liquid water. A tiny droplet of water forms around each speck of hairspray in the jar. A cloud forms.

As the droplets get bigger, you might see them raining back into the jar!

Clouds in the sky

The same thing happens to the water in puddles, lakes and oceans. The Sun heats the water. Some of the water turns into water vapour. It is carried high into the air. As the water vapour gets higher, it cools down. Tiny droplets of water form on specks of dust in the sky. The droplets gather together as clouds.

Cloudspotting

White and whispy or grey and gloomy? Clouds can be many different colours, shapes and sizes. Which of these clouds can you see in the sky?

Cirrus
The highest clouds in the sky are wispy and white. They are made from tiny specks of ice.

Altocumulus
These small fluffy clouds can be white or grey, or both.

Cirrocumulus
High in the sky, these tiny clouds make a pattern like fish scales. This is called a mackerel sky.

Altostratus
These grey-blue clouds can spread across the whole sky. Sometimes you can see the Sun shining weakly behind them.

Stratocumulus

Blue sky might peek through gaps in these flat, low layers of cloud.

Cumulonimbus

These thick, heavy clouds can be piled higher than a mountain. These are the clouds that bring heavy rain, **thunderstorms** and hail.

Cumulus

These clouds look like fluffy white sheep. If they get bigger, they can cause showers.

Nimbostratus

These thick layers of cloud block out the Sun, and can bring hours of rain or snow.

Stratus

Thick layers of cloud close to the ground make it look like the sky has been covered up with a white or grey blanket. Sometimes these clouds get so close to the ground, they become mist or fog.

Is it going to rain?

Clouds are not the only things that give us clues about the **weather**. In the past, people noticed that many plants and animals behave differently when it's going to rain.

Seagulls come inland.

Can you tell if it's going to rain? Try spotting these clues.

Cows lie down on the grass.

Deer come down from mountains to find shelter.

Dandelion and clover flowers close up.

Pinecones close.

Spiders leave their webs.

22

If swallows fly high, you'll stay dry, but if they fly low, then rain will blow!

Sheep group together and face the wind.

Cats sneeze.

Morning glories don't open their petals in the morning.

Dogs eat grass.

The louder frogs croak, the more rain you will see!

If I go to bed crowing so loud, you're sure to see rain up in the clouds!

Make a rain gauge

A **rain gauge** helps you to find out how much rain has fallen.

Toolkit

- Large plastic bottle
- Scissors
- Marker pen
- Measuring jug
- Water
- Flowerpot, soil or sand

What to do

1 Ask your grown-up to cut the neck off the bottle.

2 Take the lid off, turn the neck part upside down and rest inside the base of the bottle.

3 Measure 100 ml of tap water into the bottle. Use the marker pen to mark the water level.

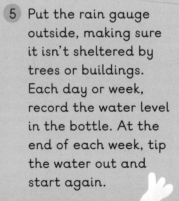

5 Put the rain gauge outside, making sure it isn't sheltered by trees or buildings. Each day or week, record the water level in the bottle. At the end of each week, tip the water out and start again.

Put your rain gauge inside a heavy flowerpot, or push it into sand or soil, to stop it blowing over.

4 Add another 100 ml of tap water and mark the water level. Keep going until the bottle is full. Then empty out the water, or use it to water the plants!

Turn a calendar into a weather chart. Each day, draw one raindrop for each 100 ml of water collected. You could draw or write down the name of the main type of clouds you spot, too (see pages 20-21).

	WEEK ONE	WEEK TWO	WEEK THREE
MONDAY			
TUESDAY			
WEDNESDAY			
THURSDAY			
FRIDAY			
SATURDAY			
SUNDAY			

Did you know?
By finding out how much rain we have had, farmers and gardeners can tell how well their plants will grow.

Make a rainbow

After rain, you might spot a rainbow in the sky. Make a rainbow of your own to find out why.

Toolkit
- Large, clear glass or plastic bowl
- Tap water
- Small mirror
- Torch (or very sunny day)
- White card

What to do

1. Fill the bowl with water.

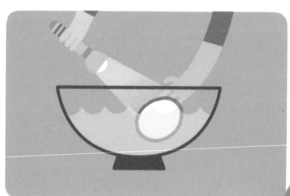

2. Holding the mirror in your hand, put it into the bowl. Shine the torch at the mirror (or move your hand around until sunlight bounces off the mirror).

3. Move the mirror around until you see a rainbow on the white card. If you don't have white card, bounce the light onto a light-coloured wall instead.

What happens?
Light slows down when it travels from air into water. This change of speed makes the light bend. Each ray of light bends by a different amount. This means that the light gets split into the colours of the rainbow. The light bounces off the mirror and travels back out of the bowl, bending again as it leaves the water.

Colours of the rainbow

Sunlight is made up of different colours of light. When they are mixed together, they make white light (it's a bit like mixing paint). When we see a rainbow, we are seeing light that has been split up into its different colours.

Red Orange Yellow Green Blue Indigo Violet

Can you spot a rainbow?

To spot rainbows on a showery day, stand with the Sun behind you. Sunlight bounces off raindrops in the sky and back towards your eyes. As the light travels in and out of the raindrops, it bends and splits up into the seven colours of the rainbow.

Try this...

A good way to remember the colours of the rainbow is to use this phrase: Richard Of York Gave Battle In Vain. It's called a mnemonic.

Snowflakes

The highest clouds are made of tiny crystals of ice. These stick together and grow into large snowflakes, which drift slowly downwards.

If the air is cold enough, snowflakes fall all the way down to the ground without melting.

Each snowflake forms around a tiny speck of dust.

A large snowball (like the head of a snowman) is made up of about a billion snowflakes!

The smallest snowflakes are so tiny, you could line up a hundred of them on a penny.

Most snowflakes are less than 1 cm across.

Land that is very high, or near the North and South Poles, gets lots of snow.

No two snowflakes are the same.

Sunshine bounces off white snow, so it can stay frozen for many days.

All snowflakes have six sides. Each of the sides is exactly the same.

Wide, furry feet stop animals sinking into the snow.

Sleet is rain that freezes as it falls. It is like a mix of rain and snow.

Many animals that live in snowy areas of the world have thick, white coats for **camouflage** and warmth.

The water cycle

The **water cycle** is the journey water takes as it moves from the land to the sky and back again. You are part of the water cycle, too.

Water vapour is light and invisible. It is carried up, up, up into the sky.

The Sun's heat turns some of the seawater into water vapour.

Pipes carry the flushed water to a sewage works. It is cleaned very well. Water is released into the sea.

Are you feeling thirsty? Turn on the tap and pour yourself a glass of water.

When you go to the loo, some of the water you drank comes out. You flush it away.

As the air cools, the water vapour turns back into tiny drops of water. These gather together as clouds.

The clouds are blown by the wind to different places. The droplets get heavier and heavier until they fall as rain, hail or snow.

The water runs across the ground into rivers and streams.

Fresh water is pumped into a water works. It is cleaned to get rid of dirt.

The clean water is piped into homes.

Did you know?
The journey of water never ends. The water you drink today may once have passed through a Tyrannosaurus rex, a Roman soldier or a royal princess!

Saving water

Water covers so much of the Earth's surface, that from space our planet looks blue! Most of this water is salt water in oceans and seas. In many parts of the world, there is not enough fresh water to go around. It is important to save water where we can.

Think about all the different ways you use water. What could you do to use less water?

Gardening
Collect rainwater in a water butt to water garden and house plants.

Precious water
Imagine that this bottle represents all the water on Earth. Just one teaspoon represents the fresh water found in clouds, rivers, **reservoirs**, lakes, ponds and underground. Just one drop is water that is available for us to use!

Washing yourself
Take a quick shower instead of a bath.

Brushing your teeth
Turn the tap off while you brush.

Flushing the loo
Check that each toilet has a water-saving device fitted.

Washing clothes
Wear clothes several times before you wash them.

Washing dishes
Rinse dishes in a sink of water, instead of under a running tap. Only run the dishwasher if it is full.

Washing cars
Use rainwater for washing cars too!

33

Make your own water filter

Water can be cleaned so that it can be used again and again.

Toolkit

- Three small plastic bottles
- Three large plastic bottles
- Water
- Jug
- Mud
- Cotton wool
- Crushed charcoal
- Pebbles
- Gravel
- Sand
- Moss
- Cleaning sponge

What to do

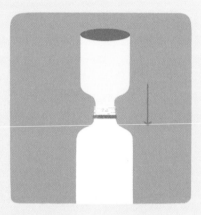

1. Ask your grown-up to help you cut the base off each small plastic bottle to make three long funnels.

2. Rest the funnels neck down inside each of the large plastic bottles.

3. Plug the neck of each funnel with a piece of cleaning sponge. Add layers of three different materials to each funnel (see page 35).

4. Mix water and mud in the jug to make dirty water. Pour an equal amount of dirty water into the top of each funnel. Wait until all of the water has trickled through.

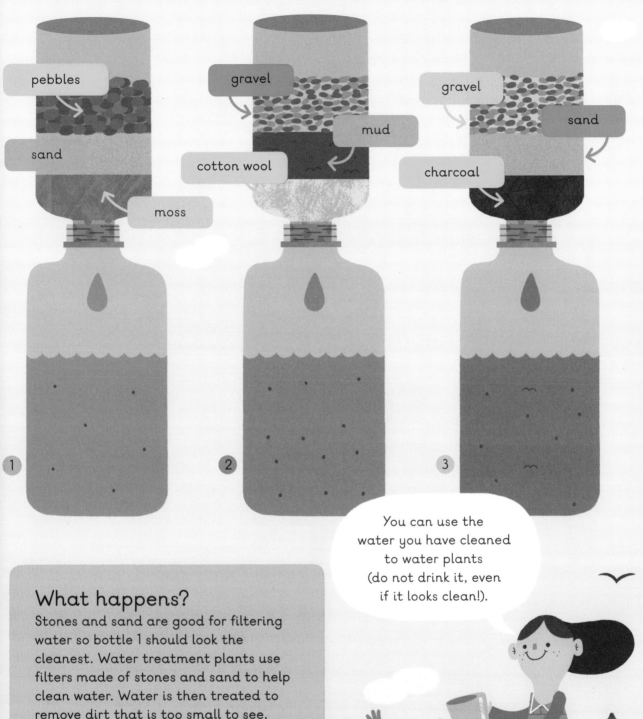

pebbles

sand

moss

gravel

mud

cotton wool

gravel

sand

charcoal

1

2

3

You can use the water you have cleaned to water plants (do not drink it, even if it looks clean!).

What happens?

Stones and sand are good for filtering water so bottle 1 should look the cleanest. Water treatment plants use filters made of stones and sand to help clean water. Water is then treated to remove dirt that is too small to see. A tiny amount of chlorine (the chemical that you can smell in swimming pools) is added to the water to stop new germs from growing in it. The clean water is piped to homes, schools and offices.

You are made of water

Water is an important ingredient in every living thing – including you! About two thirds of your body is water. Water helps your body to do many different jobs. It's important to keep it topped up!

A grown-up human body contains about 40 litres of water, and needs to be topped up with at least 2 litres of water a day. Children need to drink about 6–8 glasses a day.

Running low on water can leave you feeling weak, tired and thirsty.

The water that makes up our bodies is not pure. Many different things are mixed with or dissolved in it – including salts. This is why tears taste salty.

Saliva (spit) is mainly water. It helps you to chew and swallow food. It also helps to keep your teeth clean and healthy.

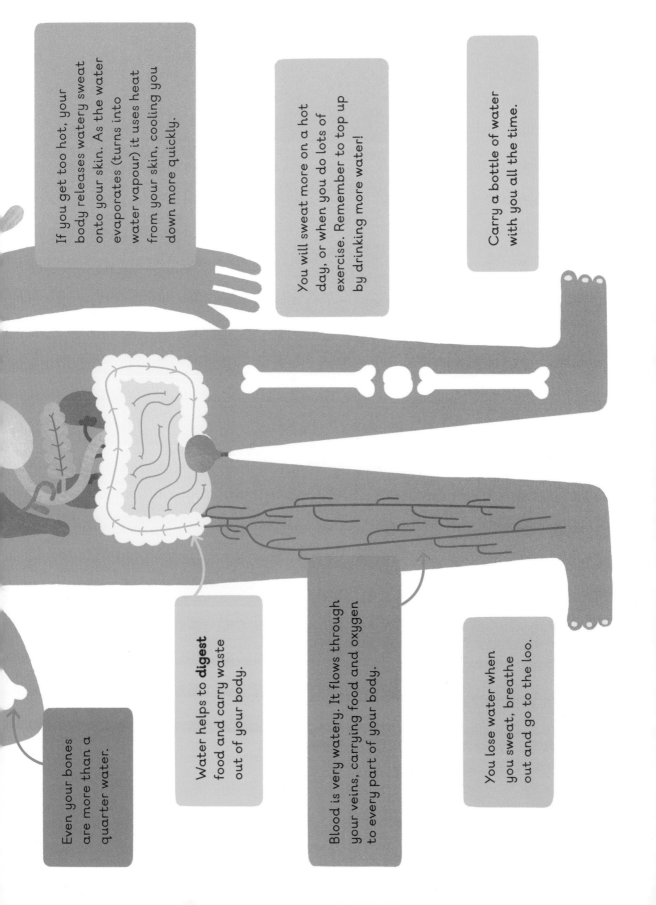

If you get too hot, your body releases watery sweat onto your skin. As the water evaporates (turns into water vapour) it uses heat from your skin, cooling you down more quickly.

You will sweat more on a hot day, or when you do lots of exercise. Remember to top up by drinking more water!

Carry a bottle of water with you all the time.

Even your bones are more than a quarter water.

Water helps to **digest** food and carry waste out of your body.

Blood is very watery. It flows through your veins, carrying food and oxygen to every part of your body.

You lose water when you sweat, breathe out and go to the loo.

Secret salt pictures

Even tap water is not completely pure. When water evaporates anything dissolved in it is left behind. You can use this to make a secret salt picture.

Toolkit

- One glass of warm tap water
- Salt
- Paintbrush
- Coloured chalk or crayon
- Paper

What to do

1 Dissolve as much salt as possible in a glass of warm tap water.

The salt disappears!

2 Use the paintbrush to paint a picture on the paper with the salty water. Leave the painting to dry.

3 Rub over the paper gently with a chalk or crayon to reveal the secret picture.

What happens?

The salt hasn't vanished – it has dissolved. This is a special kind of mixing (see page 9). The water breaks the salt up into pieces so tiny, we can't see them with our eyes. The tiny pieces spread through the water, but they are still there. When the water evaporates, the salt is left behind on the paper. When you rub a crayon over the paper, it rubs off on the rough salt and reveals your secret salt picture.

How plants use water

Green plants can make their own food.
To do this they need three things:

Sunlight

Water

Air

Leaves soak up sunlight and air.
At the same time, water escapes
through tiny holes in the leaves.
This helps the plant to suck up
more water from the roots.

Plants make food inside
their leaves. They use the
energy in sunlight to turn
carbon dioxide (from the
air) and water into sugar.
The sugar can be stored for
the plant to use later.

The stem carries water up from the roots to the rest of the plant. It also holds the leaves and flowers up!

The tip of a root is soft but it can push through tightly packed soil.

Plants suck up water through their roots. The water travels up through the stem, to every part of the plant.

Look closely at a root and you'll see it is covered in tiny hairs to help it soak up more water.

Roots also anchor plants in the ground, and soak up important minerals the plant needs.

Make a water-powered sprinkler

This garden sprinkler works using water **power**!

Toolkit

- Tall plastic bottle
- Bendy drinking straws
- Plasticine or sticky tack
- Tap water or rain water
- Jug
- Wool or string
- A grown-up helper

What to do

1 Carefully poke two small holes in opposite sides of the bottle, around 1 cm from the bottom (ask your grown-up to do this bit).

2 Push the straight end of a drinking straw into each one. Hold it in place with plasticine or sticky tack. Make sure there are no gaps around the straw. Bend the ends of the straws so they point in opposite directions.

3 Use wool or string to hang the bottle above a flowerbed or vegetable patch. Ask your grown-up to hold their fingers over the ends of the straws. Fill the bottle with water from the jug. Now take the fingers away.

What happens?

The bottle spins around and the plants get watered! Water always flows downwards. As it escapes through the straws, it pushes back on them. This makes the bottle spin. You have made an engine! It uses water power to make something go round and round.

Try this...

Try bending the straws so they point in the same direction. What happens? Can you stop the engine from spinning? Now try adding more straws. Can you make your engine spin faster?

Try adding pretty petals to your bottle, and see them spin.

Did you know?

An inventor called Hero first made engines like this more than 2000 years ago. They used steam instead of liquid water.

Make a mini pond

All animals need water, but some spend their whole lives underwater. Others spend part of their lives in water, and part on the land. Take a closer look at water creatures by making a mini pond in your garden.

Toolkit

- Spade or shovel
- Paving stones or tiles
- Large stones
- Plastic sheeting
- Water plants
- Clean sand

What to do

1. Dig a small hole in a place that gets shade and sunlight (e.g. next to a bush, but not under a tree). The hole should be deeper in the middle than the sides.

2. Line the bottom of the hole with a plastic sheet (from a garden centre).

3. Use tiles and large stones to hold the sheet in place.

4. Spread clean sand or gravel on the bottom of the pond. Buy some water plants from a garden centre, and plant them around the sides.

5. Fill the pond with rainwater. Wait to see who moves in!

Damselfly

Pond snail

Whirligig beetle

Newt larva

Diving beetle

Look out for these creatures in and around your pond. Some of them will only appear at certain times of year.

Common frog

Water boatman

Deep-sea secrets

Seas and oceans are not like enormous fish tanks, where the same creatures explore the water from top to bottom. Just like land, they contain many different habitats. The creatures you might find in a rock pool or reef are very different from those at the bottom of the deepest ocean.

Sunlight zone
0 to 200 metres

This zone is full of living things, including tiny creatures, such as algae, that use sunlight to make food for the entire ocean!

Twilight zone
200 to 1000 metres

Although some sunlight reaches the Twilight zone, it is much colder and darker than the Sunlight zone. Fish that live down here often make their own light. Large fish and marine mammals such as whales dive down from the surface to hunt.

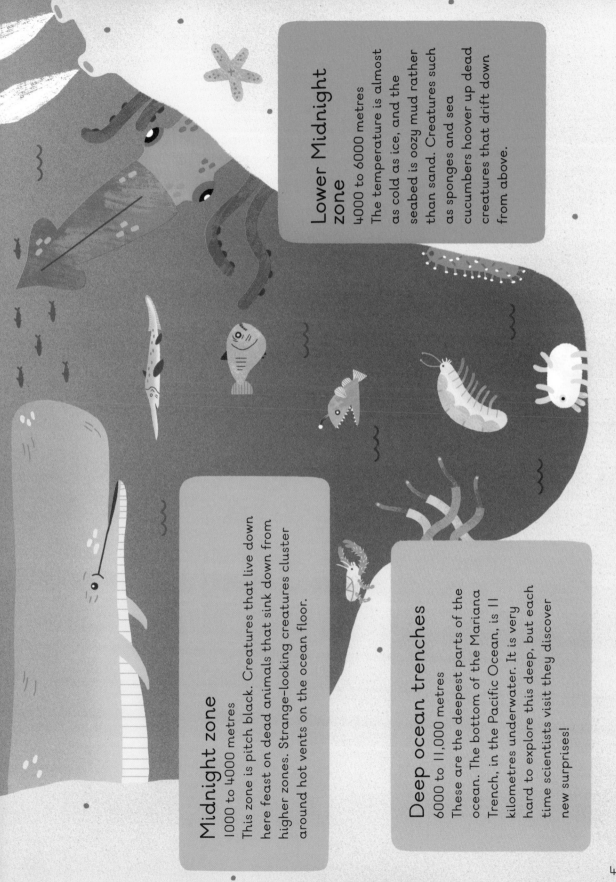

Midnight zone
1000 to 4000 metres

This zone is pitch black. Creatures that live down here feast on dead animals that sink down from higher zones. Strange-looking creatures cluster around hot vents on the ocean floor.

Lower Midnight zone
4000 to 6000 metres

The temperature is almost as cold as ice, and the seabed is oozy mud rather than sand. Creatures such as sponges and sea cucumbers hoover up dead creatures that drift down from above.

Deep ocean trenches
6000 to 11,000 metres

These are the deepest parts of the ocean. The bottom of the Mariana Trench, in the Pacific Ocean, is 11 kilometres underwater. It is very hard to explore this deep, but each time scientists visit they discover new surprises!

Life in the desert

Deserts are the world's driest places. They get less than 25 cm of rain each year, but look closely and you can still spot living things in deserts. These plants and animals have amazing features that help them to find water.

The driest deserts get no rain at all – all their water comes from fog!

Desert plants have thick stems and leaves, to trap water inside.

If a river or lake dries up, lungfish burrow into the mud and cover themselves in slimy mucus. They can survive without water for more than four years.

I bet you didn't expect to find a fish in a desert!

Hot, hot, hot!

Namibian lizards tiptoe across hot sand, standing on two legs to cool their feet. They lick drops of dew off the ground.

48

A Bactrian camel's top lip collects any snot dribbling from its nose. The snot is carried straight into the camel's mouth, so no water is wasted!

Huge roots can help desert plants collect water from deep underground. Droplets of dew run off this plant's long leaves, towards the roots.

Spikes stop birds from snacking on thorny devil lizards. The spikes also collect droplets of water from the air. The water runs off the spikes towards the lizard's mouth.

Darkling beetles face into the wind with their bottoms up in the air. Drops of water in fog collect on their wings, and run down into their mouths!

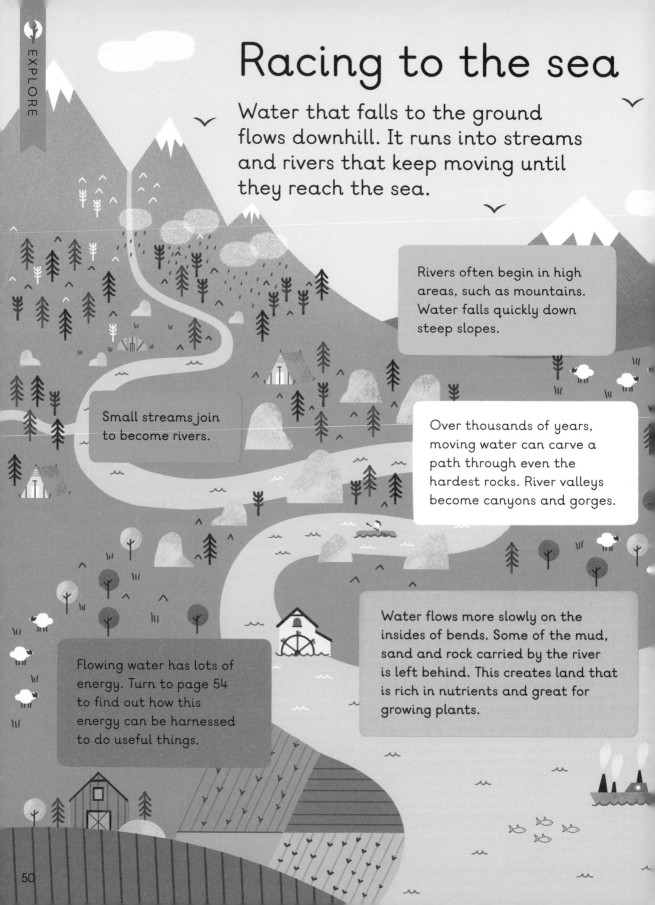

Racing to the sea

Water that falls to the ground flows downhill. It runs into streams and rivers that keep moving until they reach the sea.

Rivers often begin in high areas, such as mountains. Water falls quickly down steep slopes.

Small streams join to become rivers.

Over thousands of years, moving water can carve a path through even the hardest rocks. River valleys become canyons and gorges.

Flowing water has lots of energy. Turn to page 54 to find out how this energy can be harnessed to do useful things.

Water flows more slowly on the insides of bends. Some of the mud, sand and rock carried by the river is left behind. This creates land that is rich in nutrients and great for growing plants.

Before motors and roads, rivers were the most important type of transport. This is why towns and cities were often built near rivers, even when there is a risk of flooding.

Humans use rivers in many different ways. Some of these can change the river, and harm other animals and plants that rely on the water.

What is your nearest river called? Find out where it starts, and where it flows into the sea.

The river flows more slowly as it nears the sea. The land is usually much flatter here. As the water slows down, more of the mud, sand and rock carried by the river is left behind.

Factories are often built near rivers and seas. This can cause **pollution**, so people work to protect the world's water.

Erosion

Make a river in your kitchen to find out more about how water shapes the world around us.

Toolkit

- Sand
- Shallow plastic tray
- Jug of water
- Small twigs
- Pebbles
- Building blocks or Lego®

What to do

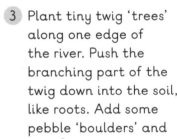

1 Fill the tray with sand and mix in a little water to make it damp (but not too wet). Press down so the sand is flat and tightly packed.

2 Use your finger to draw a winding 'river' in the sand, from one end of the tray to the other.

3 Plant tiny twig 'trees' along one edge of the river. Push the branching part of the twig down into the soil, like roots. Add some pebble 'boulders' and Lego® 'houses'.

4 Prop the tray up next to a sink. One end should be raised slightly. The other end should hang over the sink. Then slowly and gently pour water from the jug into the start of your river. Watch what happens as water flows down the river.

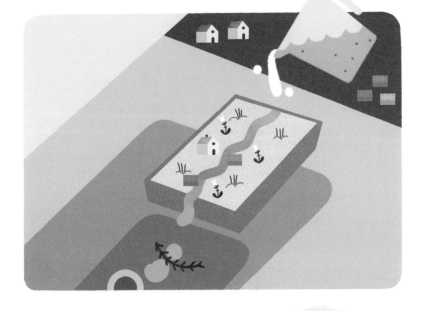

What happens?

Moving water erodes the soil around the river. **Erosion** is where land is worn or washed away by the force of moving water, wind or ice. Sometimes erosion happens quickly, for example during a flood. Sometimes it happens over thousands of years.

Did you know?

Plant roots help to hold soil in place, and stop it from being eroded. If plants and trees near rivers are cut down, land is more likely to be washed away.

Water power

People have been using the power of water to do useful work for thousands of years. Flowing water is used to turn a waterwheel, which then powers machines.

The first factories were built near rivers. Waterwheels were used to provide power for grinding wheat, or pumping water for farms.

Water always flows downwards. When it is used to turn a waterwheel, some of the energy of the flowing water is harnessed.

The flowing water pushes on the buckets and turns the wheel.

This turns the **shaft**, which is connected to a machine.

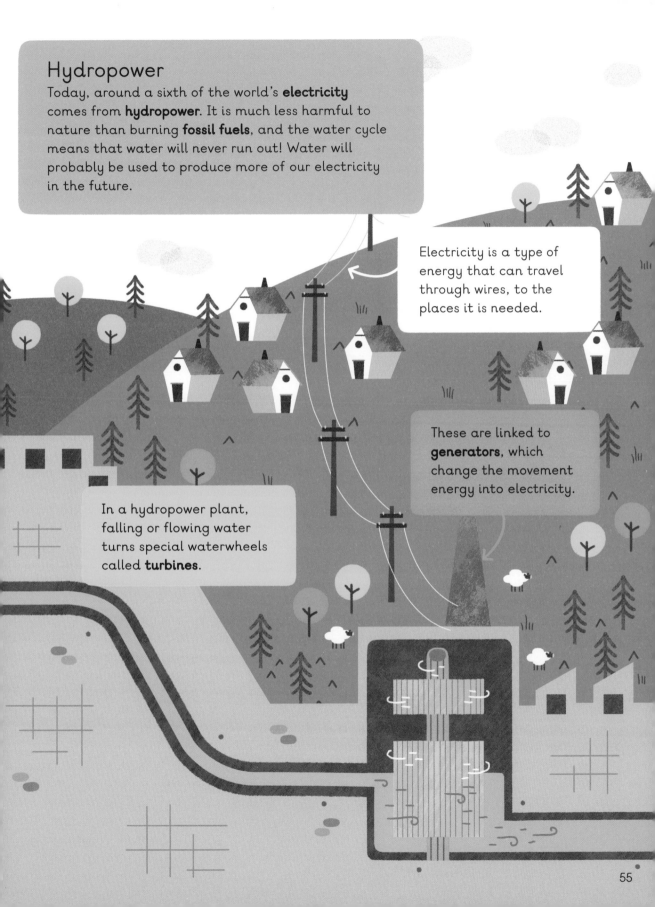

Hydropower

Today, around a sixth of the world's **electricity** comes from **hydropower**. It is much less harmful to nature than burning **fossil fuels**, and the water cycle means that water will never run out! Water will probably be used to produce more of our electricity in the future.

Electricity is a type of energy that can travel through wires, to the places it is needed.

These are linked to **generators**, which change the movement energy into electricity.

In a hydropower plant, falling or flowing water turns special waterwheels called **turbines**.

Make a waterwheel

You can make a water-powered machine at home.
Harness the energy in flowing water to turn a pinwheel.

Toolkit

- Large plastic bottle
- Wooden skewer
- Plastic carton
- Scissors
- Plasticine
- Toothpick
- Two beads that fit tightly on the toothpick
- Sticky tape
- 15 x 15 cm square of stiff paper

What to do

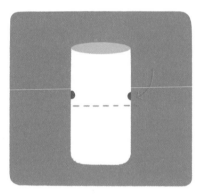

1. Ask your grown-up to cut the top off the drinks bottle, and to pierce a small hole in the centre of the lid.

2. Carefully poke two holes on opposite sides of the bottle, about halfway up.

3. Roll a plasticine sausage, around 3 cm long and 2 cm across. Then cut four rectangles of plastic from the plastic carton, each 3 cm long and 1.5 cm across. Push them into four sides of the sausage.

4. Holding the plasticine sausage inside the bottle, carefully push the skewer through the centre of the sausage and out through the other hole. Make sure the skewer can spin freely.

5 Make a pinwheel by folding the paper, as shown. Cut a line from each corner, stopping 2 cm before you reach the centre of the square.

6 Fold alternate points into the centre. Push the toothpick through all five layers of paper. Use two beads to hold the paper in place on either side.

7 Use sticky tape to fasten your pinwheel to one end of the skewer.

Make the pinwheel out of thin, waterproof plastic. See if the machine works in the rain!

8 With your thumb over the hole in the lid, fill the top part of the bottle with water.

9 Rest the top part of the bottle on the bottom part. Watch as water power makes the pinwheel spin!

Splash!

Water is not just useful – it can help us to keep fit and have fun! Which of these splashy activities have you tried?

Do you like swimming and diving?

Or zooming down slides?

Paddling, ball games or chasing the tides?

Water is fun, but it can be dangerous. Always have a grown-up with you when you go near water or try water sports.

Skiing on water – look at me go!

Or taking a peek at the creatures below?

Boarding or boating?

Surfing or sailing?

White water rafting?

Or maybe just... floating!

Water on other worlds

Scientists have sent spacecraft to look at other planets and moons in our solar system. They have spotted water in many different places.

Mars

Mars once had oceans. Ice still forms on the surface in winter, and there may be liquid water deep underground. There may have been life on Mars.

Mercury

Mercury gets very cold and probably has water ice in some places.

Earth

Earth's moon has water ice at its north and south poles.

On Earth, living things are found wherever there is water. Could there be living things in these places too?

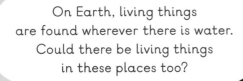

Comets

Comets are just dirty lumps of ice. As they zoom around in space, the Sun melts some of the ice, giving the comet a 'tail' of water vapour. Our water may have come from a comet that crashed into Earth billions of years ago!

Ganymede
Jupiter's largest moon, Ganymede, is bigger than Mercury! There could be liquid water below its hard crust.

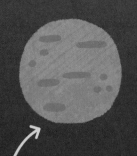

Neptune and Uranus
Both have rock and ice at their very centres.

Europa
Jupiter's moon Europa is made of ice, which may hide huge oceans of water below. Europa might have twice as much water as Earth!

Saturn
Most water in the solar system is frozen — like the lumps of ice that zoom around Saturn in rings.

Enceladus
Saturn has many moons made of ice. Enceladus has volcanoes that burp steam instead of lava. Scientists think this water might come from an underground ocean.

Mimas
Saturn's moon Mimas is one big chunk of ice, as hard as rock!

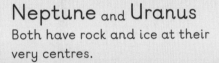

Glossary

Camouflage Colourings that allow an animal to blend in with its surroundings.

Digest Break food down so it can be used by the body.

Dissolved Broken up into pieces too tiny to see, and mixed with a liquid.

Electricity A form of energy that can travel from place to place through wires.

Erosion When soil or rock is worn away gradually by wind, rain or waves.

Evaporate Change from a liquid into a gas or vapour.

Fossil fuels Coal, oil and gas; fuels formed millions of years ago from the remains of plants and animals.

Freeze Change from a liquid into a solid.

Fresh water Water that is not salty, found in rivers, ponds, lakes and underground.

Generator A machine that produces electricity.

Hydropower Water power from the energy of falling water or fast running water, which may be harnessed for useful purposes, such as making electricity.

Melt Change from a solid into a liquid.

Pollution Damage to the natural world.

Power Energy that is being used to do something.

Rain gauge A device for measuring rainfall.

Reservoir A place where lots of water is stored.

Shaft A long rod or pole inside a machine, that transfers power from one part of the machine to another.

Steam Tiny water droplets in the air, which form as water vapour cools down.

Thunderstorm A rainstorm with thunder and lightning.

Turbine A machine that can make electricity by using wind, water, steam or gas to turn a special wheel that is connected to a generator.

Water cycle The journey of water from land to sky and back again.

Water vapour Water when it is a gas.

Weather How hot, cold, cloudy, dry or sunny a place is at a certain time.

Index

Quarto is the authority on a wide range of topics.
Quarto educates, entertains and enriches the lives of our readers—enthusiasts and lovers of hands-on living.
www.quartoknows.com

Editor: Sophie Hallam
Designer: Clare Barber

Copyright © QED Publishing 2016

First published in the UK in 2016 by
QED Publishing
Part of The Quarto Group
The Old Brewery
6 Blundell Street
London, N7 9BH

A catalogue record for this book is available from the British Library.

ISBN 978 1 78493 554 2

Printed in China